the **Wall** & the *Wind*

To Marnie Parsons. Without her, this story would have never been told.
~V.T.

the WALL & the Wind

written and illustrated

by Veselina Tomova

In the middle of the twentieth century,
in the middle of Eastern Europe, a baby girl was born.

Her family adored her:

her dad carried her around, *her mom* read her stories,

her granny sang to her, and her grandpa cherished her curls.

Soon a little brother arrived.
He was a bit annoying at first,
but quickly showed the free spirit needed
to join his big sister on grand adventures.

Together, they read about pirates and explorers.
They drew treasure maps to marvel over.

They built boats and huts and even whole harbours
in the puddle in front of the farmhouse where they grew up.

They roamed forest, field, and riverbank,
and they couldn't wait for each summer's trip to the Black Sea.
There, they camped; caught fish, mussels, and shrimp;
and joined their parents singing by the campfire.
All the songs were about love, seeking fortune,
and crossing over the horizon.

The girl was an explorer at heart; as wonderful as home was,
she longed to take off, to go beyond the fields and forests,
out, out into the wide world.

She considered running away to join the circus

or the Romani caravans

that visited her village

every summer.

But it was her ability to draw, her curiosity
and her determination to search that let her travel to strange
and wonderful lands, in her art and in her dreams.

For all her bravery,
there was one thing the girl could not do—
she could not jump over the **WALL**.

HALT
Staatsgrenze!
Passieren verboten!

The **WALL** appeared in Berlin in 1962.
It separated the East from the West,
and it was there to stay... forever.
And for everyone who lived on the East side of the wall,
life became narrow and hard.
No matter what she did,
how much she drew and dreamed,
the girl could never
jump high enough,
make a ladder long enough,
fly a balloon skyward enough,
dig a tunnel deep enough
to get past that

Then
—*unbelievably*—
almost thirty years
after the **WALL** was built,
a crack appeared.
Slowly, the **WALL** was beginning to
c
r
u
m
b
l
e

and the girl
saw a chance
to change
her life.

By now,
the girl was a mother
with a little boy of her own,
but she took that leap—
and landed, confused and hopeful,
with that wee boy,
far away from her friends and family,
far away from the life she knew,
in Canada.

On the island of Newfoundland,
with its rugged shores;
rain, drizzle, and fog;
and its wind and **Wind** and

Wind.

And now what

?

In this enormous space,
houses clung to the cliffs,
waves crashed on the shore.
Everything was exposed to the elements.
And there were no **WALLS**,
because no wall could withstand the might of the wild *Wind*.

The girl opened up her lungs and breathed in the salty air;
she squinted her eyes at the sun's sparkling reflections.

She saw that her dreams might find a fertile crack,
here, between the rocks.
The land was sparse, little more than berries and mushrooms
would grow, but there was a crispness to the air
like the promise that shimmered on a fresh canvas.

She made a home for herself and her wee boy
on a hill overlooking a harbour.
She fell in love, she drew, she painted.
Her heart soared and was broken, then it mended;
and she kept on creating.

Her house was small, but just outside, there was room
for all her old childhood desires—to sail, to explore, to discover,
and to tell her adventures with shape and colour.

She learned to make blueberry jam
and rabbit stew, and to jig for cod.
She planted a tiny garden
and cultivated a family of friends.

Meanwhile, the world changed—
boundaries shifted, borders opened,
the wall was gone at last.
The girl could return to her beloved home
in the middle of Eastern Europe,
where her brother was still minding their family farm.

And so, at the start of each planting season,
she would go back to the farm,
and take care of all the lovely tomato,

pepper,

garlic,

onion,

eggplant,

okra,

corn,

and cucumber plants,

all the herbs and flowers,
everything that grew in the land
her ancestors had worked for generations.
She would tend and she would harvest.
Her family, scattered all over the world,
would come back to reunite
and meet her friends visiting from far away.

But always she returned to Newfoundland,
pulled back to her other home,
her new world,
where she first felt
the blasting force of the wind
without a wall.

How the Book Came about

This story is based on my experience growing up in Bulgaria, behind the Iron Curtain, going to the Art School of Printmaking and Book Design in Leipzig (then Eastern Germany), and settling in Newfoundland 30 years ago, one of 3000 Bulgarians who claimed asylum in Gander in the early 1990s.

The Berlin Wall came down in 1989. As we celebrated the 30th anniversary, I couldn't stop the flood of memories, and kept thinking about the price we pay when seeking freedom and security: the families torn apart, the difficult path to re-rooting and finding belonging in a new environment.

One can be a wanderer by choice, driven by curiosity and longing to reach new frontiers, or just be tossed in the turmoil of circumstances beyond one's control and running for safety. But we all crave a place to call home. I was lucky to find mine on the rugged coast of Newfoundland, and to have the opportunity to return to my old country and reconnect with friends and family.

This book is a tribute to the wonderful people I have met on my life journey so far.

And I have been able to work with Marnie Parsons of Running the Goat, Books & Broadsides and been given the chance to do what I love: have fun with tales and images. Thank you, Marnie, this book says just that!

~Veselina Tomova

Veselina Tomova gratefully acknowledges
support for this publication from the Newfoundland and Labrador Art Council
and the City of St. John's.

ArtsNL   ST. JOHN'S

978-1-927917329

Running the Goat, Books & Broadsides gratefully acknowledges support
for its publishing activities from Newfoundland and Labrador's Department of Tourism, Culture,
Arts and Recreation through its Publishers Assistance Program; the Canadian Department
of Heritage and Multiculturalism through the Canada Book Fund;
and the Canada Council for the Arts, through its Literary Publishing Projects Fund.

Newfoundland
Labrador

Canada Council   Conseil des arts
for the Arts   du Canada

Funded by the Government of Canada
Financé par le gouvernement du Canada | Canadä

Running the Goat
Books & Broadsides Inc.
General Delivery/54 Cove Road
Tors Cove, Newfoundland and Labrador A0A 4A0
www.runningthegoat.com

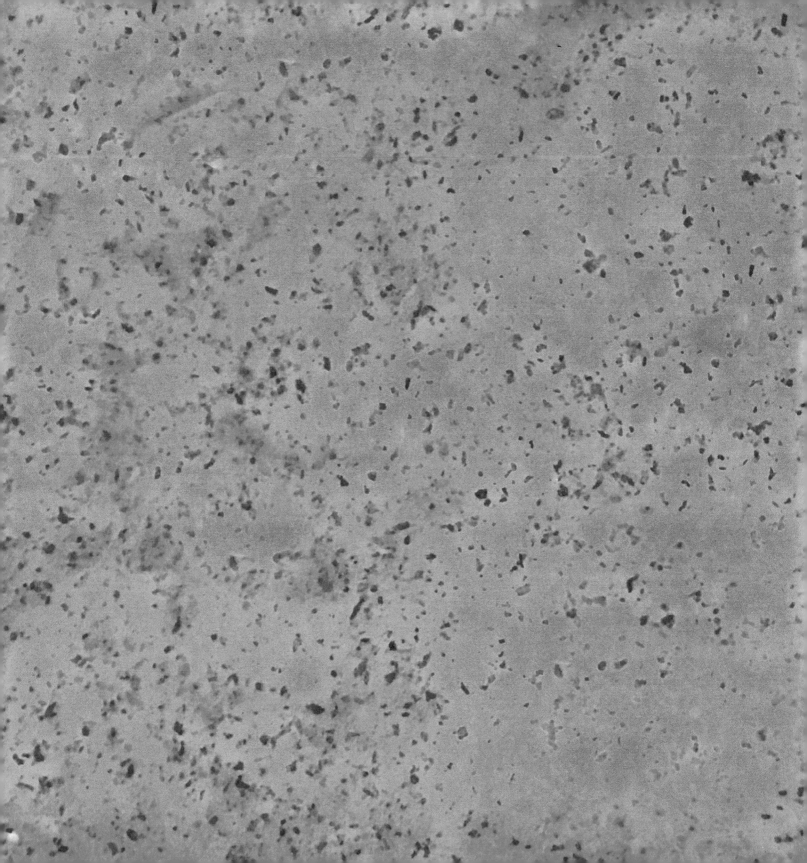